MW01532783

# HOW TO BUILD A CATERING BUSINESS

## Build a Business Collection

By

TK Johnson

Digital Edition V 1.0

Copyright 2015 by Build a Business Collection

All rights reserved. No part of this book may be reproduced by any means whatsoever without the written permission from the author, except brief portions quoted for purpose of review.

Re-selling through electronic outlets (like Amazon, Barnes and Nobles or E-bay) without permission of the publisher is illegal and punishable by law.

The scanning, uploading, and distribution of this book via the Internet or via any other means without the permission of the publisher is illegal and punishable by law. Please purchase only authorized editions and do not participate in or encourage electronic piracy of copyrightable materials.

Your support of the author's right is appreciated.

All information in this book has been carefully researched and checked for factual accuracy. However, the author and publisher make no warranty, express or implied, that the information contained herein is appropriate for every individual, situation, or purpose, and assumes no responsibility for errors or omissions. The reader assumes the risk and responsibility for all actions, and the author will not be held responsible for any loss or damage, whether consequential, incidental, and special or otherwise that may result from the information presented in this publication.

I have relied on my own experience as well as many different sources for this book, and I have done my best to check facts and to give credit where it is due. In the event that any material is incorrect or has been used without proper permission please contact me so that the oversight can be corrected.

Build a Business Collection
info@buildabusinessbooks.com

# Contents

# Introduction

I'll keep it short and sweet. This book will give you very good overview of what you will need to start and succeed in your business.

There are different ways of reading these types of books but here is the best way to read this one.

Quickly skim through it and look through the chapters. If an idea grabs you go with it and dig deeper down that rabbit hole. (Listen to the podcast if there's one on that particular topic.)

You want to keep being excited as this will be a long road.

Once you're done then get back to the beginning.

Read through the book quickly.

Read again and take notes.

Listen to the rest of the podcasts and grab your free resources. There's a chapter at the end with another link to those so no worries... you will not miss it.

*Leadership is a potent combination of strategy and character.*
*But if you must be without one, be without the strategy.*

Norman Schwarzkopf

———

*A meeting is an event at which the minutes are kept and the hours are lost.*

Unknown

———

*You are not your resume, you are your work.*

Seth Godin

———

*Beware of any enterprise requiring new clothes.*

Henry Thoreau

———

*One finds limits by pushing them.*

Herbert Simon

———

*If you see a bandwagon, it's too late.*

James Goldsmith

# Overview of Industry

The food industry is one of the biggest in the world. Aspiring entrepreneurs who love to cook are branching out and venturing into different types of food businesses such as restaurants, cafes, food trucks, catering business etc.

Catering basically involves cooking and serving special dishes for different occasions such as birthdays, weddings, meetings, and gatherings. It could be full, partial, and service only.

The catering business doesn't have to be a big one that provides meals for hundreds of people. It is always best to start small and work your way up. A small catering business is lucrative and has a lot of perks. It has a high potential for expansion and growth. This will also enable owners to focus on the important aspects

*Business opportunities are like buses, there's always another one coming.*

Richard Branson

———·.···——

*You must be the change you wish to see in the world.*

Mahatma Gandhi

———·.···——

*You only have to do a very few things right in your life so long
as you don't do too many things wrong.*

Warren Buffett

———·.···——

*The trick is in what one emphasizes. We either make ourselves miserable,
or we make ourselves strong. The amount of work is the same.*

Carlos Castaneda

———·.···——

*There's no shortage of remarkable ideas, what's missing
is the will to execute them.*

Seth Godin

———·.···——

*The great accomplishments of man have resulted from the
transmission of ideas of enthusiasm.*

Thomas J. Watson

# Daily Duties

In starting up a catering business, you must set your mind on the daily tasks that you need to do.

You catering business must have a specific style food. It could be lunch, dinner or brunch-style. Everyday, you could be cooking dishes and meals for a specific group of people. It is important to coordinate well with your customers on a regular basis to avoid confusion. 50% downpayment is usually a requirement upon signing of a contract.

Your catering business should also observe cleanliness at all times. Your utensils, cookwares, and other equipment should be sanitized.

You should also know the market demands and focus on marketing your business. You should also have your accountant to help you determine how to manage your business regarding taxes and finances. It is also important to keep records of your expenses and receipts.

## Negatives

The catering business is profitable but it is also quite challenging.

One of the challenges of being in this industry is it the stress that comes when meeting deadlines for catering business clients. Not to mention the anxiety that goes along with it when it's time to be delivered. Since your main business is food, it is perishable, so health and safety will be one of your considerations when you're in this industry.

*Everything should be made as simple as possible, but not simpler.*

Albert Einstein

---

*Far and away the best prize that life offers is the chance to work hard at work worth doing.*

Theodore Roosevelt

---

*Change is not a threat, it's an opportunity. Survival is not the goal, transformative success is.*

Seth Godin

---

*Even if you are on the right track, You'll get run over if you just sit there.*

Will Rogers

---

*You must either modify your dreams or magnify your skills.*

Jim Rohn

---

*Look well to this day. Yesterday is but a dream and tomorrow is only a vision. But today well lived makes every yesterday a dream of happiness and every tomorrow a vision of hope. Look well therefore to this day.*

Francis Gray

# Overhead

Why would I give this term its own chapter?

It is important.

It also destroys most businesses.

Very easy to allow this one to get out of control.

Overhead consists of rent, insurance, phone/internet bills, utilities, food, paper, ink, other small services, bills, charges, subscriptions, employees and everything else combined that does not look so scary when looked at individually but can add up very fast.

Keep track of it or you will regret it. Always think about how to get this down without hurting the quality of what you are selling.

# Types of Overhead Costs

To truly analyze what are the true examples of overhead costs in your business ask yourself this one question: "What must I pay for each month in order to keep my business open?"

Typical overhead expenses (sometimes referred to as fixed costs) include items such as:

- » Office Salaries
- » Employee Benefits
- » Payroll Taxes
- » Advertising
- » Stationery, Office Supplies & Postage
- » Legal and Professional Services
- » Outside Services (Performed monthly)
- » Company Car Expense
- » Dues & Subscriptions
- » Data Processing
- » Travel & Entertainment
- » Rent or Mortgage
- » Building Maintenance
- » Interest on Loans or Mortgages
- » Insurances & Taxes
- » Depreciation
- » Utilities

There are also overhead costs to consider if you have more than one department within your business.

# Types of Overhead Costs

## Departmental Overhead Costs

If you have a sales department and perhaps a shipping department, there are other examples of overhead costs to include:

- Department Specific Advertising
- Supplies
- Uniforms
- Training
- Policy Expense – This is a cost you may incur each month where a mishap occurs and you must eat the cost and should be expensed to the department where the mishap occurred.

Some businesses will include departmental wages as fixed expenses but usually only those salaries or wages that remain the same each pay period with no variation.

# Which type of business should I setup?

I know you can't wait to get your hands dirty and start making money but this step is very important. You will need to decide on a business structure. We live in a country ran by lawyers and where people love to sue each other. Due to this you should separate your personal possessions from your business. If your business goes bust or someone decides to go after you because they walked into a wall and spilled a cup of coffee on themselves it will mean that you are protected and your belongings are safe.

Most magazines recommend a sole proprietorship, a partnership or an LLC (Limited Liability Company). There other types of corporations that you can setup but for a small business starting out they are an overkill so you shouldn't worry about them now. Those other types will also cause a lot of additional accounting headaches and be more expensive to maintain.

I do not recommend a sole proprietorship. This one is the easiest as you don't actually need to file anything but gives you zero protection and a 15% self-employment tax.

Partnerships are similar except that you now allow another person into your business. You may be responsible for their mistakes and your personal items are at risk. House, car, TV... you know... the small stuff.

I'm a big fan of LLCs and recommend these the most. You have a small setup and maintenance fee but you are protected from lawsuits. This type of setup also helps with taxes and allows to deduct much more. It's a basic corporation which means that in the eyes of the law it is its own person. It can buy things, earn credit and borrow money. It is not a real corporation though which means that you can issue stock options or go public and make millions from the stock market.

Remember that the initial choice does not forfeit your rights to change later on. Times change, situations change and you can make choices more beneficial to you later on when you're good and ready.

| Type of Entity | Main Advantages | Main Advantages |
|---|---|---|
| Sole Proprietorship | Simple and inexpensive to create and operate<br><br>Owner reports profit or loss on his or her personal tax return<br><br>Simple and inexpensive to create and operate | Owner personally liable for business debts |
| General Partnership | General partners can raise cash without involving outside investors in management of business<br><br>Owners have limited personal liability for business debts | General partners personally liable for business debts |
| Limited Partnership | Owners (partners) report their share of profit or loss on their personal tax returns<br><br>Limited partners have limited personal liability for business debts as long as they don't participate in management | Owners (partners) personally liable for business debts<br><br>More expensive to create than general partnership |

| Type of Entity | Main Advantages | Main Advantages |
|---|---|---|
| Regular Corporation | Fringe benefits can be deducted as business expense<br><br>Owners can split corporate profit among owners and corporation, paying lower overall tax rate<br><br>Owners have limited personal liability for business debts | More expensive to create than partnership or sole proprietorship<br><br>Paperwork can seem burdensome to some owners<br><br>Separate taxable entity |
| S Corporation | Owners report their share of corporate profit or loss on their personal tax returns<br><br>Owners can use corporate loss to offset income from other sources | More expensive to create than partnership or sole proprietorship<br><br>More paperwork than for a limited liability company, which offers similar advantages<br><br>Income must be allocated to owners according to their ownership interests |

| Type of Entity | Main Advantages | Main Advantages |
| --- | --- | --- |
| Professional Corporation | Owners have no personal liability for malpractice of other owners | Fringe benefits limited for owners who own more than 2% of shares |
| | | More expensive to create than partnership or sole proprietorship |
| | | Paperwork can seem burdensome to some owners |
| | | All owners must belong to the same profession |
| Nonprofit Corporation | Corporation doesn't pay income taxes | Full tax advantages available only to groups organized for charitable, scientific, educational, literary, or religious purposes |
| | Contributions to charitable corporation are tax deductible | Property transferred to corporation stays there; if corporation ends, property must go to another nonprofit |

| Type of Entity | Main Advantages | Main Advantages |
|---|---|---|
| Limited Liability Company | Fringe benefits can be deducted as business expense<br><br>Owners have limited personal liability for business debts even if they participate in management | More expensive to create than partnership or sole proprietorship<br><br>State laws for creating LLCs may not reflect latest federal tax changes |
| Professional Limited Liability Company | IRS rules now allow LLCs to choose between being taxed as partnership or corporation<br><br>Same advantages as a regular limited liability company | Same as for a regular limited liability company<br><br>Members must all belong to the same profession |
| Limited Liability Partnership | Owners (partners) aren't personally liable for the malpractice of other partners<br><br>Owners report their share of profit or loss on their personal tax returns | Unlike a limited liability company or a professional limited liability company, owners (partners) remain personally liable for many types of obligations owed to business creditors, lenders, and landlords<br><br>Not available in all states<br><br>Often limited to a short list of professions |

# Where to set up your business?

If you can run your business online and I recommend you do if possible then set the company up in Wyoming. I did a lot of research on this so you're good to go. The benefits in privacy and taxes make this the right choice.

For any brick and mortar location you will need to set it up in the state that you are in.

If you are setting up a business in multiple states or live (and also do some business) in a state other than the one where you set up the original business... you might have to submit additional paperwork in that state.

Here's an example:

Let's say you setup an LLC in Illinois. You are protected and have limited liability in that state.

Your house is in Wisconsin and you have a couple of clients there. You sometimes meet with them at a coffee shop and do business in Wisconsin. You are no longer protected by the Illinois incorporation and might be breaking some state laws of Wisconsin.

If you're going to get fancy I recommend to consult with a lawyer.

*Imagination is everything. It is the preview of life's coming attractions.*

Albert Einstein

―――

*Leadership is the art of getting someone else to do something you want done because he wants to do it.*

Dwight Eisenhower

―――

*Never interrupt your enemy when he is making a mistake.*

Napoleon Bonaparte

―――

*To be successful, you have to have your heart in your business, and your business in your heart.*

Sr. Thomas Watson

―――

*Every accomplishment starts with a decision to try.*

Unknown

―――

*The first one gets the oyster the second gets the shell.*

Andrew Carnegie

# Accountants and Lawyers

You will need a lawyer to setup your business. We talk about that in a different chapter. Everything else can wait.

It's true that it is very important to have a great lawyer and a great accountant. However, that is after you're already running a profitable business and not before. These guys are a supportive team and anything they do or touch will cost you money. That is money that you cannot afford to spend when you are first starting out and trying to grow your business.

Helpful Episode:

LISTEN HERE

buildabusinessbooks.com/ep1

*Whether you think you can or whether you think you can't, you're right!*

Henry Ford

---

*A business has to be involving, it has to be fun, and it has to exercise your creative instincts.*

Richard Branson

---

*People rarely buy what they need. They buy what they want.*

Seth Godin

---

*We generate fears while we sit. We over come them by action. Fear is natures way of warning us to get busy.*

Dr. Henry Link

---

*Live daringly, boldly, fearlessly. Taste the relish to be found in competition -- in having put forth the best within you.*

Henry J. Kaiser

---

*Success is often achieved by those who don't know that failure is inevitable.*

Coco Chanel

## Business Cards and Websites

The biggest mistake I see a lot of people doing is getting the business cards and websites done before they even sell anything or get their first client. I understand that we all want to look good, be respected and appreciated.... I really do. The problem with this approach is that in itself it does not make money. It also has you focusing on the wrong things and it costs money and time. Someone will have to design your card and your websites. As someone that has dealt with designers & web site builders for a very long time and the clients getting these done... it is a pain and always takes much longer than everyone thinks.

I'd rather spend that money buying ads (whether they're online or offline), printing out flyers or doing some type of direct mail campaign. The rest of the time should be spend making calls, knocking on doors and networking.

Once you start making money and have people asking you for a business card and/or website than go right ahead. Get them done.

*A man should never neglect his family for business.*

Walt Disney

———— ◦⋅⋅⋅◦ ————

*Sometimes when you innovate, you make mistakes. It is best to admit them quickly and get on with improving your other innovations.*

Steve Jobs

———— ◦⋅⋅⋅◦ ————

*Business is more exciting than any game.*

Lord Beaverbrook

———— ◦⋅⋅⋅◦ ————

*The successful man is the one who finds out what is the matter with his business before his competitors do.*

Roy L. Smith

———— ◦⋅⋅⋅◦ ————

*The winners in life think constantly in terms of I can, I will, and I am. Losers, on the other hand, concentrate their waking thoughts on what they should have or would have done, or what they can't do.*

Dennis Waitley

———— ◦⋅⋅⋅◦ ————

*Work expands so as to fill the time available for its completion.*

Cyril Northcote
Parkinson/Parkinson's Law.

# Employees

As soon as you start making any type of money in your business then you need to start getting help. This is the fastest way to become successful. Delegation and management of others does lead to the promise land.

There are a few different ways to go about this:

**Partnerships** – Although I am completely against partners when it comes to running a business.... this is different. It's smart to package your work with other complementary offers and work with other companies to fulfill them. When this is done correctly, it can multiply your sales and theirs as you now have multiple companies selling the same products and helping each other succeed.

**Full-Time workers** – This sound like a no-brainer but hold on there just for a second professor. Anytime you hire someone full time the government steps in and sets down some pretty serious rules. A lot of it also depends on the amount of full timers but just understand that you will be paying quite a bit of taxes, unemployment insurance and possibly health care. I had a coffee shop where each full time worker cost me double. Their salary and another that went to the government. The details are beyond the scope of this book but keep this in mind.

**Part-Time workers** – I like these. Hopefully with systems in place they are replicable. No over time for part timers and not much hassle when it comes to making changes. You will pay some taxes but don't worry about unemployment of healthcare.

**Consultants** – These can be helpful for some things but not recommended. Some examples of them are Accountants, Lawyers, Marketing companies, SEO companies, Web Designers, Cleaners etc. Use them only when you need to but do not rely on any too much. If the SEO Company is in charge of all your leads... you do not have a business.

**Freelancers/Contractors** – Good for one of jobs. If you are not a brick and mortar and can work location independent... these guys can be your "full time" and "part time" staff (but obviously don't say that out loud to anyone).

This way you give them a 1099 and they are treated as a business expense. Love this.

**Interns** – If you can get someone to work for a pizza, a dream or a school credit... do it. Keep in mind that they do need extra training and watching over but this is where systems come in.

**Outsource** – You've probably heard about Virtual Staff. The workers in the Philippines, India, Romania that power most of the international companies. They are great and not as expensive as the US work force. Anything that does not need to be done face-to-face with a customer (and as long as the US law doesn't disallow it) can be outsourced. Some tasks might be under some kind of a privacy act which does not allow the information to leave your actual office. The payments are usually done via PayPal and can be treated as an expense. Also a win and a topic that is beyond the scope of this book.

Helpful Episode:

LISTEN HERE

buildabusinessbooks.com/ep2

*I feel that luck is preparation meeting opportunity.*

Oprah Winfrey

---

*Ideas in secret die. They need light and air or they starve to death.*

Seth Godin

---

*The true entrepreneur is a doer, not a dreamer.*

Unknown

---

*My son is now an 'entrepreneur'. That's what you're called when you don't have a job.*

Ted Turner

---

*The man who will use his skill and constructive imagination to see how much he can give for a dollar, instead of how little he can give for a dollar, is bound to succeed.*

Henry Ford

---

*For all of its faults, it gives most hardworking people a chance to improve themselves economically, even as the deck is stacked in favor of the privileged few. Here are the choices most of us face in such a system: Get bitter or get busy.*

Bill O' Reilly

# Interview Process

Here are some tips that I've learned while hiring.

It's more important to have an honest, punctual and competent person than a skilled applicant. Obviously you will not be hiring someone that doesn't know anything for a skilled position. However, if you have a group of people applying that pass the minimum requirements then always focus on the personality rather than a fat resume and good recommendations (which can all be faked). Being late and other small negative behavior traits are a good window into the future.

The best way to find out if a person is right for the job is to have them work on something and watch how they do.

The best interview questions are open ended. Ask about opinions, why they think a certain way and what they would do in certain situations rather than about their past accomplishments and how they would describe themselves. Keep in mind that there are coaches and books that get people ready for the most common questions. If you ask the things that all other employers ask for... you will see a performance.

In your job ad make sure to put a very small detail that will show if the applicant is actually paying attention or shooting out resumes by the hundreds. Example: Please post the words 'purple rainbow' in the header of your e-mail next to your name and position you are applying for. If they can't do that much... don't expect a good employee.

*Please think about your legacy, because you're writing it every day.*

Gary Vaynerchuck

---

*Victory goes to the player who makes the next-to-last mistake.*

Savielly Grigorievitch Tartakower

---

*I like thinking big. If you're going to be thinking anything, you might as well think big.*

Donald Trump

---

*Surviving a failure gives you more self-confidence. Failures are great learning tools... but they must be kept to a minimum.*

Jeffrey Immelt

---

*To think is easy. To act is difficult. To act as one thinks is the most difficult.*

Johann Wolfgang Von Goeth

---

*Yesterday's home runs don't win today's games.*

Babe Ruth

# Personality Tests

I have found that it is much more important to hire a person with the personality than the best skills. This does not mean that you should not hire someone that has skills. I simply mean that skills can be learned while a personality cannot be changed. Also whenever you have two people applying for the same position with similar skillsets... always chose the better personality.

Some of this can be judged by your gut feeling. Hopefully if you're not the one doing the interviewing then the person that is doing it looks for the same things you're looking for.

I also found some awesome personality tests that you can give out to the potential employees.

Here's the link:

GRAB YOUR FREE RESOURCES HERE

buildabusinessbooks.com/freeresources

*Please think about your legacy, because you're writing it every day.*

Gary Vaynerchuck

---

*Victory goes to the player who makes the next-to-last mistake.*

Savielly Grigorievitch Tartakower

---

*I like thinking big. If you're going to be thinking anything, you might as well think big.*

Donald Trump

---

*Surviving a failure gives you more self-confidence. Failures are great learning tools... but they must be kept to a minimum.*

Jeffrey Immelt

---

*To think is easy. To act is difficult. To act as one thinks is the most difficult.*

Johann Wolfgang Von Goeth

---

*Yesterday's home runs don't win today's games.*

Babe Ruth

# Payroll

Should you pay people yourself?

It depends.

There are two parts to this and a twist.

Writing a check to an employee or paying in cash is simple. That's part one.

Calculating all of the taxes and who gets them on what you just paid is not. This is when you would probably want some help. I've used a company called ADP before and they were good without being over-expensive. There are others so shop around. You submit the hours and amounts that the worker is getting and they take care of the rest.

Here's the twist.

Freelancers, Contractors or Outsourcers have to pay their own taxes and worry about that. You simply pay and mark down how much you paid in your expenses.

# Average Salaries

How much the catering business makes depends on various factors such as its business structure, its location, the demand and number of clients.

A caterer in the U.S. earns an average salary of $18,570 annually. Depending on some factors, caterers could earn up to $51,125 annually.

# Job Ads

Here are examples of catering jobs online.

# Lead Catering Attendant (Catering / U Club)

**Apply Now**

## About Aramark

Aramark (NYSE: ARMK) is in the customer service business across food, facilities and uniforms, wherever people work, learn, recover, and play. United by a passion to serve, our more than 270,000 employees deliver experiences that enrich and nourish the lives of millions of people in 22 countries around the world every day. Aramark is recognized among the Most Admired Companies by FORTUNE and the World's Most Ethical Companies by the Ethisphere Institute. Learn more at www.aramark.com or connect with us on Facebook and Twitter.

### Responsibilities
### Essential Tasks and Responsibilities:

- Oversee and assist in preparation of food items for the day and dating products
- Oversee and assist in setting up and breaking down of stations designated by the manager
- Cook and otherwise prepare foods according to recipes and directions
- Responsible for use of correct portions when preparing and serving items on the line
- Maintain daily temperature logs
- Responsible for taking samples of all food items on the line prior to serving the customers
- Alert management and pull food items that do not meet quality expectations
- Complete opening and closing station checklists
- Greet customers as they approach and leave the serving line
- Ask customers about the quality of their service and handle any complaints (with assistance from the manager on duty) while maintaining a positive attitude and smile
- Oversee and assist in maintaining a clean work station (including floors, work areas, equipment, walls, refrigerators, and meat blocks)
- Ensures that all work areas and serving utensils are cleaned and sanitized
- Responsible for proper disposal of waste from the service line
- Transfers supplies and equipment between storage and work areas by hand or by cart
- Assist with daily STEP observations and report safety hazards discovered in the location to management immediately

## Sales & Catering - Catering Services Coordinator - Georgia Gwinnett College

Apply Now

### About Aramark

Aramark (NYSE: ARMK) is in the customer service business across food, facilities and uniforms, wherever people work, learn, recover, and play. United by a passion to serve, our more than 270,000 employees deliver experiences that enrich and nourish the lives of millions of people in 22 countries around the world every day. Aramark is recognized among the Most Admired Companies by FORTUNE and the World's Most Ethical Companies by the Ethisphere Institute. Learn more at www.aramark.com or connect with us on Facebook and Twitter.

### Responsibilities

**Job Summary:** The Catering Supervisor is responsible for supervision and support in planning catering events of varying sizes and levels in both central and satellite locations. Ensures that all catering brand standards and initiatives are consistently achieved.

### Essential Tasks & Responsibilities:

- Develops and is accountable for a safety culture that creates a work environment where no one gets hurt. Directly supervises catering operations including such duties as coordination of staff and rental equipment, set-up, preparation, service, and break down of catered foods, beverages, and events of varying size and complexity.
- Booking of events, selecting and costing menu items, and pricing as needed.
- Assists with hiring, discipline, and performance reviews.
- Coordinates activities with other internal departments. Participates in management team meetings. Interfaces with vendors and key service users within client organization.
- Facilitate external customer relations; represents Aramark and the client at any and all meetings and events.
- Ensures that appropriate sanitation, organization, and safety standards are met through the use of checklists, hands-on supervision, and follow-up.
- Participates in all catering training programs; helps to develop and implement training programs for hourly, part-time, and student employees.
- Aid in implementation and adherence to all Aramark OpX Catering initiatives and guidelines.

### Qualifications

- Minimum of two years operational experience in a hotel/banquet setting required.
- Prior experience with booking of events preferred.

# CATERING ATTENDANT- GAME DAY CATERING - CINCINNATI SPORTSERVICE AT GREAT AMERICAN BALL PARK (CINCINNATI, OH)

DNC - ♀ Cincinnati, OH

Posted: 8/8/2015

Food and Beverage: Server/Concessions
CATERING ATTENDANT- GAME DAY CATERING - CINCINNATI SPORTSERVICE AT GREAT AMERICAN BALL PARK (CINCINNATI, OH)
JOB TITLE: CATERING ATTENDANTJOB CODE(S): 1371JOB FAMILY: FOOD & BEVERAGEFLSA STATUS: NON-EXEMPT

UNIT SPECIFICUNIT NAME: CINCINNATI BASEBALLREPORTS TO: GAME-DAY CATERING MANAGERUNION/NON-UNION: UNIONPAY RANGE: EVENT PAYSHIFT/HOURS REQUIRED: VARIES (APPROX 5-7 HOURS PER SHIFT)AGE REQUIREMENT (IF APPLIC): MUST BE 19 YEARS OF AGE OR OLDER/ MUST BE 21 YEARS OF AGE OR OLDER TO HANDLE LIQUOR

POSITION SUMMARYUnder direction of supervisor, ensures effective operation of assigned catering areas, including stocking, serving and attending to guests' needs, in accordance with Company's GuestPath Universal Service Standards and applicable Operational Standards.

ESSENTIAL FUNCTIONS:• Sets up and checks on assigned catering areas prior to event, to ensure proper items are in place, in accordance with company procedures• Verifies and sets-up all pre-event food and/or beverage orders• Takes and places event-day food and beverage orders• Set-ups and checks on event-day food and beverage orders• Replenishes food, beverages, condiments and utensils as needed• Maintains standard of orderliness and cleanliness of catering area throughout the event• Obtains signatures from the host on charges (if applic)• Serves guests until the end of the event• Clears all items from the area and cleans all surfaces and chafing dishes in area• Re-sets and re-stocks area for next function• Completes closing functions and checks out with supervisor• Performs other duties as assigned.

NON-ESSENTIAL FUNCTIONS:

EDUCATION & EXPERIENCE:• Minimum of 6 months to 1 year of service experience in a hotel, full service restaurant, catering facility or club environment required;

KNOWLEDGE, SKILLS & ABILITIES:• Excellent guest service skills; ability to adhere to Company's GuestPath Universal Service Standards• Ability to complete required pre-employment sanitation and alcohol service training• Organizational skills; detail-oriented• Ability to work accurately, efficiently, and courteously in a high pressure environment.• Good communication skills; ability to effectively communicate with guests, and retain and communicate menu information and service preferences• Ability to follow job procedures and supervisor instructions• Basic math skills; ability to accurately account for cash and inventory.

# Systems

This is my favorite part and I can't recommend it enough to start building up systems from day one. A good rule is this: If you can do it and you do it often... and it makes you money than you shouldn't be doing it yourself.

If you do not take this advice then keep this in mind. You will spend a lot of time working in the business and not on the business. That's because you will be too tired to do so. You will also have a very hard time managing employees, scaling and finding new opportunities.

There are thousands of stories out there of people who set out to build a business in order to get money and freedom. Let's leave aside the startups that you see funded on Shark Tank by Venture Capital. Most of those will never make the owner money and an entire book could be written just on those. To sum it up though... in those types of businesses the founder is looking to make some revenue and grow (might never make profit) and sell to a bigger firm that wants them (either because their business can complement what the larger one is doing, they have an idea how to monetize it better or they want the competition gone).

Back to what you're building...

The business person quickly finds out that there is simply too much to do. He becomes responsive and becomes very reactive. The hours disappear and he can barely get his work done. The overwhelm and burnout hits him and he realizes that he does nothing more but work. Forget family and friends. Also the money is not there. Then a competitor comes and makes things even harder. Let's hope he doesn't go too much into debt. You get the picture.

On the other side of the coin you have a company like McDonalds that has amazing systems. Crappy food but amazing systems.

They know how to find a location. Almost every one of their franchises makes money if not all of them. They can train the new owner quickly. The employees do not need to possess any types of skills and can be replaced easily. Everyone knows their tasks, roles and exactly what is expected of them.

It's a much different experience running a business with systems than without.

I recommend some great books on this topic later on.

Helpful Podcast Episode:

LISTEN HERE

buildabusinessbooks.com/ep3

*The golden rule for every business man is this: Put yourself in your customer's place.*

Orison Swett Marden

———

*To win without risk is to triumph without glory.*

Pierre Corneille

———

*People don't believe what you tell them. They rarely believe what you show them. They often believe what their friends tell them. They always believe what they tell themselves.*

Seth Godin

———

*A successful man is one who can lay a firm foundation with the bricks others have thrown at him.*

David Brinkley

———

*Instead of wondering when your next vacation is, you ought to set up a life you don't need to escape from.*

Seth Godin

———

*I had to make my own living and my own opportunity! But I made it! Don't sit down and wait for the opportunities to come. Get up and make them!*

C.J. Walker

# Productized Services

I want you to consider the following two scenarios very carefully:

Scenario #1 – A client comes in and asks for you to do a job. You ask them what they want and they start rattling off the different parts and components of the job. You do not want to lose them but know that this type of a custom job will take a lot of planning and be quite expensive. After all, someone has to pay the bills. You agree. After a while you figure that this is more complicated and harder than you previously thought. The couple of hours of research now turn into days and if you were honest with yourself and counted it all... you'd realize that you are starting to match the salary of a fast food worker. You call the client and say that it will take a bit longer and might cost more but they're pissed and don't want to hear it. You finish it, and hand it off to a now disgruntled customer while only making a couple of bucks.

Scenario #2 – A client comes and asks you to do some work for them. You show them a set menu list of the types of things you offer. It always starts with all the bells and whistles included but as they start objecting about money you simply look at them and say "what would you like for me to take off?" People hate losing things much more than they want to gain and so the customer huffs and puffs but takes almost everything. You know exactly how long it takes you to complete these jobs and the margins you have. Easy sale without much thinking involved.

That my friends is the difference between a custom job and a productized service. We have already spoken about systems in a previous chapter and let me ask you "which one do you think will be easier to scale and make money on?"

In order to get ready for Scenario #2 you will have to put in more work. You will have to complete the task and measure the time/cost/materials and write each stop down so that the next person can copy you. Don't worry. Nobody will steal your business from you... especially not your employee who would never withstand the responsibility of running the show. Even if they do... you can tweak the system, hire new people and leave them behind. This is the road to freedom.

The point here is to not have to think and re-shape the wheel for every customer. If you draw the line in the sand early on there won't be any whining/changing things/complaining later on.

Helpful Episode:

LISTEN HERE

buildabusinessbooks.com/ep4

*People are best convinced by things they themselves discover.*

Ben Franklin

———

*I don't pay good wages because I have a lot of money; I have a lot of money because I pay good wages.*

Robert Bosch

———

*Opportunity is missed by most people because it is dressed in overalls and looks like work.*

Thomas Edison

———

*Everyone is a genius. But if you judge a fish by its ability to climb a tree, it will spend its whole life believing it is stupid*

Einstein

———

*Do or do not. There is no try.*

Yoda

———

*Your most unhappy customers are your greatest source of learning.*

Bill Gates

# Location

I assume you're already aware of this but location is everything. If you don't have foot traffic or eye balls that means that you have to find all of your customers. This is normal for large companies who set up offices somewhere in a cheap location and send sales people on the streets to hit offices door to door or have a team of cold callers.

You can do the sales yourself and there's nothing wrong with that but do not fall into the trap of making your first hire a sales person if you don't know how to sell anything yourself. It will destroy your business. That person will never care as much about your business as you do and will hold too much power over you.

Here is a list of tips to help:

- The city's zoning laws might allow for your kind of business in that area.
- The existing utilities should be up to code and adequate. Upgrading those on day one is not good.

- The lease/rent need to be reasonable. It's a part of your monthly overhead. Don't underestimate it.
- Employees are willing to come to your neighborhood. Hopefully you can find them right around the block because they live there. Safety and low crime rates are key.
- Also check insurance as it varies based on neighborhoods.
- Same with the customers. Rarely will someone drive out of their way to pay for anything. You're not the DMV, IRS, Welfare or an Immigration Office. They choose the worst locations on purpose.
- The area shouldn't depend on seasonal traffic. Vacation towns suck.
- Who is next door? Can you borrow their customers? Are they going to hang in for a while or are looking to run as soon as the lease is over? Introduce yourself and ask some questions. It's ok. They won't bite.
- We all drive cars. Look at the parking situation.

I prefer working from home, co-working spaces or coffee shops. It gives me more control over my time and location and most clients never know the difference. Also it creates a much smaller overhead and that money can stay in my wallet or go into the marketing budget.

*Leadership is doing what is right when no one is watching.*

George Van Valkenburg

---

*In the business world, everyone is paid in two coins: cash and experience. Take the experience first; the cash will come later.*

Harold Geneen

---

*Those who say it can not be done, should not interrupt those doing it.*

Chinese Proverb

---

*Whatever the mind of man can conceive and believe, it can achieve. Thoughts are things! And powerful things at that, when mixed with definiteness of purpose, and burning desire, can be translated into riches.*

Napoleon Hill

---

*To succeed in business, to reach the top, an individual must know all it is possible to know about that business.*

J. Paul Getty

---

*A consultant is someone who takes the watch off your wrist and tells you the time.*

Unknown

# Healthcare

Here is how the Affordable Care Act (also called "Obamacare") impacts an average small business. For the sake of this discussion a small business has 25 or less employees. Anything above would be labeled as a "medium" or a "large" business.

You will need to:

1. Provide the employees with a notice that educates them about the Health Insurance Marketplaces. This will differ depending on the state. Inform that they might get a tax credit if purchasing their insurance through one of these marketplaces. Inform that they may decide to switch from the employer chosen insurance to the one of their choosing.
2. Increase Medicare withholding on the salaries. If you have read the other chapter you will know that I recommend for a 3rd company to take care of the payroll. These changes happen often and

it is simply too much to keep track of it and too easy to get in trouble by missing something.

3. The health insurance must be offered within 3 months of the employee joining. Previously some companies made the new hires wait longer until they could sign up for a company plan.

These rules apply to full time workers and is one of the reasons why so many corporations have been switching to part time workers, contractors and freelancers.

Further Reading:
https://www.sba.gov/content/employers-with-fewer-25-employees

*The only way around is through.*

Robert Frost

---

*The new source of power is not money in the hands of a few, but information in the hands of many.*

John Naisbitt

---

*The critical ingredient is getting off your butt and doing something. It's as simple as that. A lot of people have ideas, but there are few who decide to do something about them now. Not tomorrow. Not next week. But today. The true entrepreneur is a doer, not a dreamer.*

Nolan Bushnell

---

*You miss 100 percent of the shots you don't take*

Jeffrey Immelt

---

*Successful people are the ones who are breaking the rules.*

Seth Godin

---

*To the degree we're not living our dreams; our comfort zone has more control of us than we have over ourselves.*

Peter McWilliams

# Requirements

In starting up a catering business, it is important to follow and meet some requirements.

First, you must have a menu to offer your clients. Write a business plan because small business administration asks for a business plan that contains the structure, market analysis, as well as maintenance cost. Set clear plans and target sales. It is also important to plan your marketing strategy.

You must obtain the necessary business permit to operate. Requirements and regulations depend on where you live. You will also have to secure a sanitation permit because it is a food industry.

Find the perfect location for your business. Look for areas where there are great opportunities for your business. Purchase the necessary utensils, equipment, wares for your catering business.

Like most entrepreneurs do, it is always smart to insure your business. You may talk to your insurance agent regarding business insurances. You should also ensure its security by hiring security officers that will look after your shop.

*The absolute fundamental aim is to make money out of satisfying customers.*

John Egan

---

*If you would like to know the value of money, try to borrow some.*

Benjamin Franklin

---

*If it really was a no–brainer to make it on your own in business there'd be millions of no–brained, harebrained, and otherwise dubiously brained individuals quitting their day jobs and hanging out their own shingles. Nobody would be left to round out the workforce and execute the business plan.*

Chinese Proverb

---

*Get busy living or get busy dying.*

from the "The Shawshank Redemption"

---

*Winners take time to relish their work, knowing that scaling the mountain is what makes the view from the top so exhilarating.*

Denis Waitley

---

*Statistics suggest that when customers complain, business owners and managers ought to get excited about it. The complaining customer represents a huge opportunity for more business.*

Zig Ziglar

# Taxes

I predict a ton of interesting conversations that you will be having with your accountant but here's the one that comes up the most.

"I'm paying too much in taxes. The government is killing me here. What can I deduct or write of as a business expense?"

In the section I will list most of the 'legal' expenses that you can do. There's a reason I say this as you would be surprised some of the things that people try to write off.

*Saying no to loud people gives you the resources to say yes to important opportunities.*

Seth Godin

—

*To think creatively, we must be able to look afresh at what we normally take for granted.*

George Kneller

—

*Business in a combination of War and sport.*

Andre Maurois

—

*To succeed... You need to find something to hold on to, something to motivate you, something to inspire you.*

Tony Dorsett

—

*Always forgive your enemies. Nothing annoys them more.*

Oscar Wilde

—

*All paid jobs absorb and degrade the mind.*

Aristotle

# Expenses

List of the most common expenses.

Turn the page.

## Typical Business Expense Categories

*Which ones will be applicable to your business?*

» Accounting/bookkeeping, and financial consulting fees
» Advertising expenses
» Amortization
» Automobile expenses (only the percent that is used for business)
» Bad debts that you cannot collect
» Bank service charges and fees
» Board meetings
» Books and periodicals
» Building repairs and maintenance
» Business/trade conventions
» Business travel
» Business gifts (annual limit of $25 per recipient)
» Business meals (50% is deductible)
» Cafeteria health-insurance plan (requires plan)
» Charitable deductions made for a business purpose
» Cleaning/janitorial services
» Coaching fees, if related to your business
» Collection Expenses
» Commissions to outside parties
» Computer, printer, and software (if used over 50% for the business)
» Consultant fees
» Conventions and trade shows
» Costs of goods sold
» Credit card convenience fees

# Typical Business Expense Categories

*Which ones will be applicable to your business?*

- Depreciation and amortization
- Discounts to customers
- Dues for professional and trade associations
- Education expenses for maintaining or improving required skills (Yourself & Employees)
- Email, Internet access, and web hosting services
- Employee wages
- Entertainment for customers and clients
- Equipment & repairs
- Exhibits for publicity
- Family member wages
- Fax machine
- Franchise fees (new)
- Freight of shipping costs
- Gifts for customers ($25 deduction limit for each) – recommend gift cards over cash
- Group insurance (if qualifying)
- Health insurance
- Home Office (not recommended)
- Insurance expense
- Interest
- Investment advice and fees
- Legal and attorney fees
- License fees and taxes

## Typical Business Expense Categories

*Which ones will be applicable to your business?*

- Losses due to theft
- Management fees
- Materials
- Maintenance
- Merchant account or credit card processing fees
- Mortgage interest on business property
- Moving
- Newspapers and magazines
- Office furniture, fixtures and equipment
- Office supplies
- Online services used for the business
- Outside services
- Parking and tolls
- Payroll taxes for employees (Social Security, Medicare & Unemployment taxes)
- Parking and tolls
- Pension plans
- Postage and shipping
- Publicity
- Printing and duplication
- Prizes for contests
- Real estate – related expenses
- Rebates on sales
- Rent (business or during business travel)

## Typical Business Expense Categories

*Which ones will be applicable to your business?*

» Research and development
» Retirement plans
» Royalties
» Safe-deposit box
» Safe
» Self-employment taxes
» Storage rental
» Subcontractors
» Start-up expenses (amortized over 60 months)
» State and local business taxes
» Preparation of business tax return
» Telephone expense (only for a separate business line)
» Travel expenses
» Utilities
» Website design
» Workers' compensation insurance

# Audits

Here are the two main reason for getting the IRS to knock on your door and want to bend you over the table.

These are tips given to me by two different but amazing accountants.

1. Do not write off your home as a business expense. Things get very complicated here and usually throw up a red flag with the IRS. You will need to calculate the square feet used for business. How much time you spend there. The percentage of the utilities etc.

2. The IRS does not have a large work force and can only handle a small number of cases per year. What usually happens is that when they find someone that has been cheating on their taxes they will then go after the accountant who has completed that paperwork. It's not that this person will get in too much trouble that should worry you but something bigger. Their book of business. This is what the government wants. It's a way for

them to get a lot of easy wins which they love. Anytime you hear an accountant that is a little too creative walk away. You could be stepping on a land mine.

*Winning is not a sometime thing; it's an all time thing. You don't win once in a while, you don't do things right once in a while, you do them right all the time. Winning is habit. Unfortunately, so is losing.*

Vince Lombardi

———

*There is no security on the earth, there is only opportunity.*

General Douglas MacArthur

———

*Never put off until tomorrow what you can avoid altogether.*

Unknown

———

*Hire character. Train skill.*

Peter Schutz

———

*For maximum attention, nothing beats a good mistake.*

Unknown

———

*Early to bed and early to rise probably indicates unskilled labor.*

John Ciardi

# Marketing

In order to market to a customer, it helps to know who that perfect customer is.

Few sample questions to ask yourself:

- How old are they?
- What are their interests?
- What's the gender?
- How educated are they?
- Do they have kids?
- Do they own a home?
- What kind of car do they drive?
- What is their average salary?

Answering these questions will give you a better idea of who this person is. Now you can go ahead and craft your message. The more in-tune you are the less your marketing budget needs to be.

Let me explain one more thing. There are two different types of marketing. One is to get a sale and the other is to build brand awareness. Leave the brand building to the big companies for now. If you do have the budget for brand building... initially focus on one channel only.

For example: Local newspaper.

It will take weeks, if not months, of a person seeing your ad to even notice it. It will take even longer for them to become familiar with it and to start trusting it. After all you're starting to re-appear for a long time so you are not going anywhere. People like that. It will take even longer than that for them to actually remember you and call you. The process could take a year for each person. You never know when they start seeing your ad and whether they have a need for your service. Brand building is hard.

Not all advertising/marketing takes this long.

Here are some examples of marketing on a budget:

**Flyers** – These can be distributed around the area of your business or on a parking lot of a competitor. I'd say to keep it clean but you could potentially do that. Mailboxes or behind car windows make a good leaving spot. You can also hire a person to hand them out if you have a lot of foot traffic on the block.

**Posters** – Get them up in windows, on street corners or at the free advertising boards (such as the ones seen at entrances to most supermarkets or coffee shops). If you can offer something free to reel in the potential clients... even better.

**Upsells** – I already mentioned that it's a good idea to partner up with other businesses who sell similar products or services. Let me add to that. It is also great to have a free offer such as a consultation after which you can pitch your paid services. You might also have a tripwire which is a very low cost product that establishes trust between you and the customer making it easier to sell to them. It could be a trial offer (for a few dollars), a book or something else that you've seen others doing in your industry. Many of these are actually loss leaders. It's something worth more than you are selling it for but it hooks the person on wanting more of it from you. Bottom line is that these work great.

**Referrals/word of mouth** – Other businesses refer you. Customers refer you. This is something you will have to put some work in and build the right relationships. Also whatever you're selling needs to be good.

**Follow-Up** – Most companies drop the ball here. The sale is made and no one contacts the same customer again. There's a saying that your best future customer is your current customer. It costs much more to buy a new customer that it is to sell to a current one. It doesn't have to be the same offer.

**Cold-Calling** – This is my least favorite but it works. The problem with it is that you are throwing the net out very wide without a clue on who's around. It's a numbers game. Usually if you try and sell a 100 people something then one will end up buying it. Could be that they feel sorry for you but they will. If conversions are any lower than that, you are in trouble.

The Internet – Get me to the number one spot in Google and I will conquer the world. I've heard that one before. SEO takes a long time to work and is hard. It's unstable. It is a strategy that can break at any time. Google cannot be controlled and I like to think that it hates us. After all they make money through paid advertising only and not the free search. Look into ppc (pay per click) or at least combine it with SEO for quicker results.

It doesn't matter which of these methods you choose but it does matter that you measure the results. Stop doing things that do not work. I admit that having a show on YouTube is good for the ego but does it make you money?

*Don't worry about people stealing your ideas. If your ideas are any good, you'll have to ram them down people's throats.*

Howard Aiken

———

*It takes more than capital to swing business. You've got to have the A. I. D. degree to get by —— Advertising, Initiative, and Dynamics.*

Ren Mulford Jr.

———

*A calm sea does not make a skilled sailor.*

Unknown

———

*The worst part of success is to try to find someone who is happy for you.*

Bette Midler

———

*Your time is precious, so don't waste it living someone else's life.*

Steve Jobs

———

*Only when the tide goes out do you discover who's been swimming naked.*

Warren Buffett

# Networking

There is no secret to effective networking. It is something that can be developed and learned. Networking is also a tool to market your business and there are things that anyone who plans to start up a business should be aware of.

So what are the dos and don'ts in networking?

**Do your homework**. It is important to actually know what you are saying. Confidence follows when you are well prepared because you'd be able to answer questions headed your way.

**Provide Business Cards**. Business Cards are necessary to exchange contact numbers and details. Make sure that you have plenty so you won't need to worry about running out of them, especially during meetings.

**Do Listen**. Listening is an important part of networking. You are not making conversations just for sales pitch, but you also need to listen and learn from other people you meet.

**Be Patient**. Developing relationships takes time. People who are impatient tend to ruin business deals and relationships.

**Do not limit yourself to one person**. Speak to plenty of people. Making connections is very important for effective networking.

**Do not forget to follow up on your clients**. They might be just as busy as you are or even busier, so making follow-ups are very necessary to maintain business relationships.

**Create a Twitter or a Facebook Account**. These days, social networking is a powerful tool in bridging a gap or creating channels.

**Maintain a friendly image**. Who wants to talk to someone who comes across as arrogant?

Here's a link for further listening:

LISTEN HERE

buildabusinessbooks.com/ep5

# Seminars & Conferences

Here are some seminars or trainings you may go to:

http://www.nace.net/

https://bus.wisc.edu/about-us/conference-services/catering-menus

http://www.unicen.cam.ac.uk/conference-and-events/event-conference-catering

http://www.unh.edu/conferences-catering/

# Linkedin Pages

https://ph.linkedin.com/company/bunzl-catering-supplies

https://www.linkedin.com/company/global-gourmet-catering

https://www.linkedin.com/company/bakersbestcatering

https://www.linkedin.com/company/broadway-gourmet?trk=extra_biz_viewers_viewed

# Other Networking Opportunities

https://www.facebook.com/UsaCateringRosangel

https://www.facebook.com/lancercatering

https://www.facebook.com/McCallsCatering

https://www.facebook.com/PoloCafeAndCatering

# Profit

If you can't make a profit you will go out of business. When looking at income reports on the internet from some of the more known marketers it's funny that they only speak about revenue. It means nothing. It's the same on the show called "The Profit". Many businesses that are making over a million in sales are still in debt. It's crazy.

Always focus on the bottom line.

One of the worst things to do is to sign up for a ton of monthly services. Carpet cleaning, SEO, forums, magazines etc...

These all look harmless individually but when grouped can really eat into what you will get to keep.

Another piece of the puzzle is the actual cost of production. Whether you're creating a physical product or performing a service it is crucial to understand the exact cost of it. Whether its supplies, electricity and/or time. They both cost money. If you do not have this part down then you cannot price things properly. It's impossible to have a healthy margin otherwise.

A margin is the difference between what you make the product for and what you sell it for. It's the money that you pay for your overhead and that you get to keep.

The overhead would be things such as the building, utilities not used for production, other employees, insurance etc...

It's also a good idea to break down your overhead into daily chunks. That way you know exactly how much you need to make per day to not go into debt.

Further Watching:

WATCH HERE

cnbc.com/live-tv/the-profit

*Your income is directly related to your philosophy, NOT the economy.*

Jim Rohn

---

*The NBA is never just a business. It's always business. It's always personal. All good businesses are personal. The best businesses are very personal.*

Mark Cuban

---

*Fire the committee. No great website in history has been conceived of by more than three people. Not one. This is a deal breaker.*

Seth Godin

---

*Once you free yourself from the need for perfect acceptance, it's a lot easier to launch work that matters.*

Seth Godin

---

*You have brains in your head. You have feet in your shoes. You can steer yourself, any direction you choose.*

Dr. Seuss

---

*It is not the strongest of the species that survive, nor the most intelligent, but the one most responsive to change.*

Charles Darwin

# Margins

On the next couple of pages you will find the average profit margins broken down by each industry.

| Industry | Number of Firms | Net Margin |
|---|---|---|
| Advertising | 52 | 3.98% |
| Aerospace/Defense | 93 | 7.64% |
| Air Transport | 22 | 9.32% |
| Apparel | 64 | 7.46% |
| Auto & Truck | 22 | 3.16% |
| Auto Parts | 75 | 3.44% |
| Bank (Money Center) | 13 | 18.9% |
| Banks (Regional) | 676 | 22.23% |
| Beverage (Alcoholic) | 22 | 14.21% |
| Beverage (Soft) | 46 | 12.66% |
| Broadcasting | 28 | 11.56% |
| Brokerage & Investment Banking | 46 | 12.48% |
| Building Materials | 39 | 4.09% |
| Business & Consumer Services | 177 | 4.29% |

| Industry | Number of Firms | Net Margin |
| --- | --- | --- |
| Cable TV | 18 | 9.31% |
| Chemical (Basic) | 46 | 5.98% |
| Chemical (Diversified) | 10 | 7.43% |
| Chemical (Specialty) | 103 | 10.01% |
| Coal & Related Energy | 42 | -4.44% |
| Computer Services | 119 | 5.56% |
| Computers/Peripherals | 64 | 13.69% |
| Construction Supplies | 55 | 6.14% |
| Diversified | 23 | 10.12% |
| Drugs (Biotechnology) | 400 | 11.18% |
| Drugs (Pharmaceutical) | 151 | 15.95% |
| Education | 42 | 1.99% |
| Electrical Equipment | 126 | 5.64% |
| Electronics (Consumer & Office) | 28 | 3.56% |

| Industry | Number of Firms | Net Margin |
|---|---|---|
| Electronics (General) | 189 | 6.18% |
| Engineering/Construction | 56 | 1.56% |
| Entertainment | 84 | 12.59% |
| Environmental & Waste Services | 103 | 3.08% |
| Farming/Agriculture | 37 | 3.33% |
| Financial Svcs. (Non-bank & Insurance) | 288 | 34.14% |
| Food Processing | 96 | 6.87% |
| Food Wholesalers | 14 | 1.79% |
| Furn/Home Furnishings | 27 | 3.98% |
| Green & Renewable Energy | 26 | 0.36% |
| Healthcare Products | 261 | 9.49% |
| Healthcare Support Services | 138 | 2.16% |
| Heathcare Information and Technology | 127 | 6.72% |

| Industry | Number of Firms | Net Margin |
|---|---|---|
| Homebuilding | 35 | 6.82% |
| Hospitals/Healthcare Facilities | 56 | 4.50% |
| Hotel/Gaming | 80 | 3.72% |
| Household Products | 135 | 8.99% |
| Information Services | 67 | 13.78% |
| Insurance (General) | 24 | 8.47% |
| Insurance (Life) | 25 | 8.19% |
| Insurance (Prop/Cas.) | 52 | 9.00% |
| Investments & Asset Management | 148 | 19.11% |
| Machinery | 137 | 8.54% |
| Metals & Mining | 124 | 1.63% |
| Office Equipment & Services | 25 | 4.47% |
| Oil/Gas (Integrated) | 8 | 9.99% |
| Oil/Gas (Production and Exploration) | 392 | 7.52% |

| Industry | Number of Firms | Net Margin |
|---|---|---|
| Oil/Gas Distribution | 85 | 3.04% |
| Oilfield Svcs/Equip. | 161 | 3.81% |
| Packaging & Container | 26 | 4.90% |
| Paper/Forest Products | 22 | 2.58% |
| Power | 82 | 8.03% |
| Precious Metals | 147 | -13.91% |
| Publshing & Newspapers | 43 | 13.54% |
| R.E.I.T. | 213 | 19.01% |
| Real Estate (Development) | 18 | 1.26% |
| Real Estate (General/Diversified) | 11 | 34.38% |
| Real Estate (Operations & Services) | 52 | 4.96% |
| Recreation | 68 | 8.69% |
| Reinsurance | 4 | 8.52% |
| Restaurant/Dining | 79 | 9.40% |

| Industry | Number of Firms | Net Margin |
|---|---|---|
| Retail (Automotive) | 30 | 3.12% |
| Retail (Building Supply) | 5 | 6.00% |
| Retail (Distributors) | 90 | 4.23% |
| Retail (General) | 23 | 2.67% |
| Retail (Grocery and Food) | 21 | 2.71% |
| Retail (Online) | 46 | 2.34% |
| Retail (Special Lines) | 128 | 3.46% |
| Rubber& Tires | 4 | 3.16% |
| Semiconductor | 100 | 13.70% |
| Semiconductor Equip | 47 | 4.73% |
| Shipbuilding & Marine | 14 | 13.96% |
| Shoe | 13 | 8.95% |
| Software (Entertainment) | 20 | 10.11% |
| Software (Internet) | 327 | 15.57% |

| Industry | Number of Firms | Net Margin |
|---|---|---|
| Software (System & Application) | 259 | 17.34% |
| Steel | 40 | -4.33% |
| Telecom (Wireless) | 21 | -2.93% |
| Telecom. Equipment | 126 | 14.51% |
| Telecom. Services | 77 | 11.47% |
| Tobacco | 20 | 22.42% |
| Transportation | 21 | 4.96% |
| Transportation (Railroads) | 10 | 18.29% |
| Trucking | 30 | 3.78% |
| Unclassified | 8 | -43.05% |
| Utility (General) | 21 | 8.71% |
| Utility (Water) | 19 | 15.03% |
| Total Market | 7887 | 7.84% |

# Public Relations

PR basically means free advertising.

Imagine that you just bought a newspaper. On one page you see an article on a new company that is very inspiring and doing thing differently in your town/city. They might be treating the employees differently, paying higher wages, and giving longer vacation or allow its people to work from home/coffee shops or abroad. You flip a few more pages and you see a huge ad. This one shows that there is a sale at a flower shop. There's a few word and a nice picture but you barely think of it and move on. Later on there is another article but it says paid advertising on the bottom or top. It talks about the benefits of a new supplement. The article is very dry and you get bored after one paragraph.

The difference here is that the first one cost that business nothing while the other two were paid for and were most likely not cheap. Getting a full page or two in any newspaper is not cheap. Also most of us have a case of ad blindness and no longer respond well to them. It takes a lot of impressions (times the person views an ad) before they even realize it.

Where the first article could be stuck in your mind because you had an open mind while reading it.

Hiring a PR firm might not be in your budget or worth it. However contacting the local news does make sense if you have something to talk about. Remember that all of them need constant things to talk about.

Helpful podcast episode:

LISTEN HERE

buildabusinessbooks.com/ep6

*The golden rule for every business man is this: Put yourself in your customer's place.*

Orison Swett Marden

---

*To win without risk is to triumph without glory.*

Pierre Corneille

---

*People don't believe what you tell them. They rarely believe what you show them. They often believe what their friends tell them. They always believe what they tell themselves.*

Seth Godin

---

*A successful man is one who can lay a firm foundation with the bricks others have thrown at him.*

David Brinkley

---

*Instead of wondering when your next vacation is, you ought to set up a life you don't need to escape from.*

Seth Godin

---

*I had to make my own living and my own opportunity! But I made it! Don't sit down and wait for the opportunities to come. Get up and make them!*

C.J. Walker

# Customer Management

There's no better client than the one you already have paying the bills. You need to keep track of them, continually communicate with them and keep them happy.

Here's a great episode on how to do this:

LISTEN HERE

buildabusinessbooks.com/ep7

It also touches on upselling and the tools to use for customer retention management. It also gives some great insights into what you need in place first before even trying to set up a system from which you can manage your existing clients.

*The only place success comes before work is in the dictionary.*

Vidal Sassoon

---

*Speak the truth, but leave immediately after.*

Unknown

---

*The important thing is not being afraid to take a chance. Remember, the greatest failure is to not try. Once you find something you love to do, be the best at doing it.*

Debbi Fields

---

*Are you a serial idea-starting person? The goal is to be an idea-shipping person*

Seth Godin

---

*The problem with the rat race is that even if you win, you're still a rat.*

Lilly Tomlin

---

*Success in business requires training and discipline and hard work. But if you're not frightened by these things, the opportunities are just as great today as they ever were.*

David Rockefeller

## Additional Resources

I'm continually researching and compiling lists of the best available apps/habits/tricks/tips and anything else I can find on how to level up and grow as a person and how to expand my business.

This could be articles/links/books/videos/movies etc... (I don't discriminate)

You can get the most current version of that list here: FREE RESOURCES

buildabusinessbooks.com/freeresources

*If you work just for money, you'll never make it, but if you love what you're doing and you always put the customer first, success will be yours.*

Ray Kroc

———— ⚜ ————

*Long–range planning works best in the short term.*

Doug Evelyn

# MASTERMINDS

This is the closest to a silver bullet or magic sauce that you will get to. One of the ways that I've seen businesses grown faster and smarter is when the owner joins a Mastermind.

A mastermind is a group of people from a similar field and with different levels of experience that meet on a regular basis and help each other grow. This is not a referral swap, meetup with a bunch of people trying to sell each other something or some other pyramid scheme. We've all attended plenty of those so do not get confused.

The point of the meeting is to address the problems that each member is dealing with at that exact moment. New walls crop up all of the time as we grow. When we're in the middle of the battle it is nice to get advice from someone that is looking at it from a hill above. Each person has a couple of minutes to explain what they are struggling with and the rest of the group gives suggestions or advice. The process can take 15-20 minutes or the entire mastermind.

I've seen it work both ways. Each person gets their problem solved or each week the group goes in-depth into someone's business.

Another huge component of this is the accountability. Not only do we have others around that understand what we are going through but after we commit to an action... during the next meeting the group will question us about it.

The last benefit and most likely the biggest is the friendships formed. Your network can grow very quickly through these types of masterminds. Unfortunately it's not that easy to form new ones and some do get stale after a while. Best ones consist of people from different industries so that you can get completely fresh insights and with people that you don't previously know.

The guys that created the movie "Your Own Way Out" came out with a very interesting idea and I was able to work out a deal with them.

*(The movie shows an entire movement of people who are writing their own scripts and regaining*

*freedom while growing their networks and businesses. It's very cool. )*

They are organizing rotating masterminds. This means that every few weeks you join a new group. This gives a ton of eyeballs a shot at your business problems. Your network grows on steroids and the groups never get boring or old.

The offer can be found here: www.yourownwayout.com/special-books-offer/

SPECIAL DISCOUNT CODE: WINNER-N8

# Leave a Review to Win a Kindle

## Click Here to Win a Kindle

buildabusinessbooks.com/review

68264358R00061

Made in the USA
Lexington, KY
06 October 2017